The **Little Fish Guide** to **Networking**

How to make
word-of-mouth
marketing
work for you

Jackie Barrie

Also by Jackie Barrie
The Little Fish Guide to DIY Marketing (2010)

Published by Comms Plus
ISBN 978-0-9565933-2-0

"One of the critical aspects of networking is that you stop blaming the tools and start looking toward yourself. Praise yourself if you are achieving referrals and develop yourself if you are not. I have seen and heard many tales of woe and tales of joy inside all networks, whether online or offline. Networking is not just a skill, it is an attitude of mind. Jackie's style of networking (just be friendly and nice) is a good fit with Ecademy's open, random and supportive philosophy. Her approach works, and her tips will be invaluable to any small business that wants to include networking as a route to market. Her psychology experience means she knows how people tick. Her writing experience means the book is an easy read. And her marketing experience means it's packed with practical advice to help you get results. [This book] would be a great help to people starting out on their journey."
Penny Power, Founder of Ecademy and Ecademy Digital School

"In her typically clear and uncluttered style, Jackie's books and articles never fail to inform and hold the interest of the reader - the Little Fish Guide to Networking is no exception. As "Big Boss" (Jackie's words!) of 1230 The Women's Company – a networking organisation supporting both the career woman and those with their own businesses – I'm pleased to confirm that Jackie's guide to networking is both entertaining and spot on!"
Jackie Groundsell, 1230 The Women's Company

"The Little Fish Guide to Networking should be on the 'must read' list for anyone running a small or medium sized business. If you're already a networker I challenge you not to find a few nuggets of wisdom that will make your networking more successful and if you're not a networker yet because "it's scary" or "I'd be no good at it", Jackie's brilliantly readable guide will de-bunk such myths. As the founder of a networking organisation, I hope all my members will read this book – because I'm sure they'll get a better return from their networking investment if they do."
David Thackray, Founder, Venture Catalyst

With thanks to all the networkers
who have helped me grow my business so far
– I hope I've given as good as I've got!

Contents

Foreword by Andy Lopata

Sometimes one single connection can have a huge impact on the future direction of your business.

In 2003 I was Managing Director of Business Referral Exchange Networking (BRX) and Jackie Barrie was an Area Partner, organising groups in South London for us. Jackie called me one day to tell me that she was putting on an event to promote our group in Croydon, and that I should come along. She had invited a guest speaker and she thought that I would be interested in meeting him.

I put the date in my diary and Jackie introduced me to the speaker beforehand. We arranged to meet in the Hilton Hotel in Croydon a couple of hours before the event. The meeting was with Peter Roper, who was at the time the President of the West Midlands Chapter of the Professional Speakers' Association (PSA)*. Although I had given a handful of presentations up to that point, I was unaware that you could be paid to speak, let alone make giving presentations a core part of your business. Jackie had seen me speak and train and could see the value I would get from meeting with Peter.

Little did she know! I joined the PSA a couple of months later and started speaking more widely as a result. I went on to become a vice-president of the PSA and speak in front of large audiences and big corporations internationally. I also co-authored two books through people I met in the PSA, including '...and Death Came Third!', which peaked at Number Two in the Amazon Top 100 on launch.

*Now Professional Speaking Association

The co-author of '...and Death Came Third!'? Peter Roper.

By introducing me to Peter, Jackie changed the course of my career. Jackie has that invaluable skill of seeing where valuable connections lie for other people and making sure she makes the match. She is a committed networker and was one of our most treasured team members when I was with BRX.

Jackie Barrie has been networking with commitment, intelligence, humour and passion for nearly a decade now. She understands what is needed to ensure that you add value to your network and to ensure that your network is valuable for you.

Much of that experience and the lessons Jackie has learnt are laid out in this book. It's a great guide for anyone starting out in the often confusing world of networking. Listen to her advice and learn from her experience.

Andy Lopata
Business Networking Strategist
"One of Europe's leading business networking strategists" - The Financial Times
Andy's new book, 'Recommended: How to Grow Your Business Through Referrals and Networking" will be published in the summer of 2011 by Financial Times Prentice Hall.

What's this book about?

Face-to-face communication remains one of the most powerful ways of doing business.
Source: BusinessEurope.com

When I'd just started out, I asked a good friend of mine who'd been freelancing as a copywriter for a few years: "How do you find your clients?" I don't remember her exact answer, but I do remember feeling slightly dissatisfied. She didn't really tell me how to find clients. They just seemed to find her.

After running Comms Plus since 2001, I now get 98% of my work from repeat and referral business. And when people ask me the same question, I feel as though I don't provide a satisfactory answer to them either. Somehow, clients just seem to find me. And I reckon that's because of all the effort I've put into building a brand and reputation locally (and because I provide a superb service that plenty of people really want, of course). I've achieved this success through networking, a.k.a. face-to-face marketing.

So what qualifies me to write a book about networking? Well, I have been Area Partner for eight BRX groups across south-east England, with responsibility for up to 70 members at one time. I was also co-moderator of the Croydon Ecademy club in its first two years, and co-founded the Bromley Creative Community. I have organised events from networking meetings to a prestigious conference for 200 senior managers and a fun fundraiser for the Save the Children Fund. I have no vested interest in networking; I am a business-owner who generates almost all my work through word-of-mouth.

I practice what I preach.

I find networking a great way to win clients (and suppliers, joint venture partners and friends).

Top tip: It's good practice to ask 'How did you hear about us?" and record the source of all new enquiries so you know what marketing works best for you.

Through networking (online and offline), I am booked to capacity most of the time. It's ironic, as traditional marketing is the main service I provide to my clients, yet I do so little of it for myself.

When you start or run your own small business, you're like a little fish in a big pond (and you need to learn all the tricks so you can avoid the sharks).

In my series of Little Fish Guides, you can find everything you need to know about marketing on paper, on screen and in person, backed up by stories and examples from my own experience of 30 years in the industry.

'Sales' is noticing the signals that show when a customer is ready to buy and actually doing the deal.
'Marketing' is attracting the right customers in the first place (at the right time and for the right price).

If you would like more information about DIY marketing, social media or business writing, please contact me at jackie@comms-plus.co.uk.

If you want to know how to market your business via word-of-mouth (a.k.a. 'networking'), read on...

Jackie Barrie

What is face-to-face marketing?

Sometimes effective communication can't be achieved by a piece of paper or on screen, it just has to happen face-to-face.

When you have an important message to communicate, you may decide to present it in an informal meeting, a formal presentation or an interactive workshop. You may wish to build your perceived expertise by offering yourself on the guest speaker circuit. Event managers are crying out for experts to share their knowledge. Sometimes they even pay you! Other times, you get exposure to an audience who may book appointments later. You can sell your products at the back of the room ('you've heard the speech, now buy the book!'). At the very least, you can invite audience members to sign up to your newsletter. That way they're hooked. You email them regularly (don't you) so they remember you exist and you are the first person they think of when they (or someone they know) needs your service.

If, like me, you are in the kind of business that depends on who you are, then you need to do some networking to get yourself known and to meet a lot of people.

Quality v Quantity debate
Some networking experts believe the more people you meet, the more money will naturally flow your way through the random connections you make. Others (including me) believe networking works best when you make fewer, but deeper relationships. As with most things, the real answer may well be a bit of both.

Networking works (when you do it right)!

In one week I was working on 15 projects. Of those, 12 came from people I met through formal networking and three from people I know through informal networking.

Traditional marketing takes more money than time. Word-of-mouth marketing (or networking) takes more time than money. Scrimping on either one won't work.

However, you still need marketing materials to back it up and build brand recognition, such as brochures, leaflets, newsletters and websites. If you are in the kind of business that doesn't depend on who you are, then you don't need to network, you can rely on advertising and other marketing instead.

People buy from people

The sales person is a key determinator of purchase. Appearance, personality, charisma, confidence, rapport, enthusiasm all play a part. When you go networking, you are your own salesperson.

Extracts from a manual written by David Ogilvy for AGA's 1935 advertising campaign, that still hold true today (mostly):

In general, study the methods of your competitors and do the exact opposite.

The worst fault a salesman can commit is to be a bore... and if you can make her laugh you are several points up.

Find out all you can about your prospects before you call on them... Every hour spent in this kind of research will help you and impress your prospect.

Perhaps the most important thing of all is to avoid standardisation in your sales talk. If you find yourself one fine day saying the same things to a bishop and a trapezist, you are done for.

The more prospects you talk to, the more sales you expose yourself to, the more orders you will get. But never mistake a quantity of calls for quality of salesmanship.

The good salesman combines the tenacity of a bulldog with the manners of a spaniel. If you have any charm, ooze it.

Routes to market

Whether you are a small business, sole trader or just starting out, you need to find customers before you make any money. But you probably have a limited marketing budget, if you have one at all. So how do you get people to know you exist? They won't buy your stuff – product or service – if they don't know you are there.

As with anything, if you want to get something out (customers), you have to put something in (time, money, energy).

You can't afford to do what the big boys do. They have a massive spend on routes to market including advertising, direct mail campaigns and telemarketing.

Exercise

List all the big brand names you can think of e.g. Levi's, Coca Cola, Virgin, McDonalds ...

_____
_____
_____
_____
_____
_____
_____
_____
_____
_____

Bet you've seen their adverts on TV, on racing cars, at bus-stops – often in all of those places and more. They are trying to build brand recognition, to ensure customers think of them first. You will probably have seen or heard the same ad a few times. That's because it takes up to 18 viewings for a brand to 'fix' uppermost in your mind.

Some more numbers: You might need to contact a 'cold' prospect 7-9 times before they notice you e.g. postcard, letter, direct mail. A stranger might need up to 29 such 'touches' to become a client.

Top tip: Whatever marketing you do, you have to do it repeatedly to get results.

A question of balance

Smaller businesses need to balance the time/cost/quality equation. You can't have all three. You can either have a service that's cheap and quick but poor quality, or top quality at a good price but slow, or fast and good but pricey. Although it would be ideal to position yourself in the middle of the Venn diagram below, there's always a trade-off.

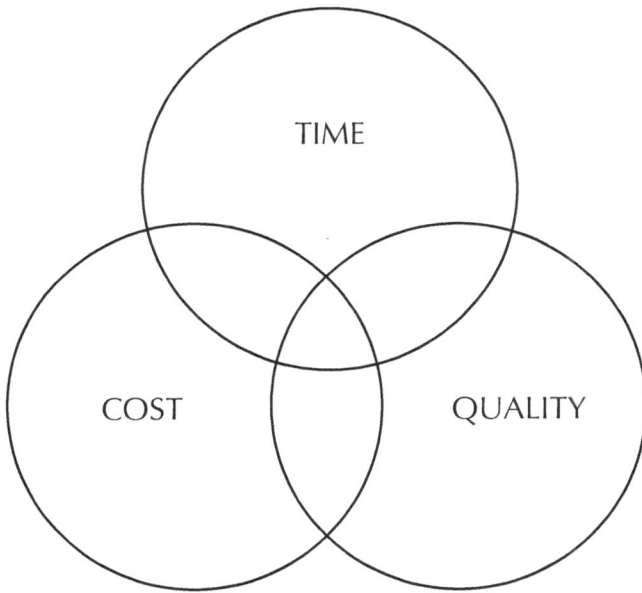

Small businesses tend to have more time than money. Big businesses tend to have more money than time. Either way, you want good quality results.

In the early stages, you probably have more time than money (because you haven't found any customers yet).

If you are NOT a big brand name, people buy from you because of Who You Are not because of What You Are Called. No-one buys from the big boys because of who works there. They buy because of their brand name. That's why it's worth the big fish investing in advertising (which costs more money than time), while the little fish need to invest in word-of-mouth marketing (which takes more time than money).

It doesn't necessarily take a lot of money to build a reputation and get your business known. It certainly can take a lot of time. You have to get out there and meet people, because it's not who you know, it's who knows you!

Top tip:
Brands advertise, SMEs* network.

●━━━━━━━━━━━━━━━━━━━━━━━━━━●

SMEs	Big brands
Invest time	Invest money
Networking	Advertising
Sell because of	Sell because of
who they are	what they are called

*SME stands for Small or Medium Enterprise

Horses for courses

A telecoms provider had heard that networking is a good route
to market, and invested a lot of time and energy in membership
and organisation of different groups. He attracted a few low value
referrals in the early years, but then it went quiet. He asked me
why networking wasn't working for him any more.

We discovered that his business had grown to the stage where
it attracted big corporate clients (those who don't go out
networking; they don't need to). They bought from him, not
because of who he was as an individual, but because of the brand
identity and service levels he'd developed.

In his case, advertising would provide a better ROI*. He didn't
have the time to go networking any more. He did have the money
to pay for ads to appear in the media that his clients favoured.

The more you give, the more you receive
The more matchmaking you do, the more matches will be made
for you
The more knowledge you give away, the more you will learn
The more you invest, the more you will earn

Source: 'Networking for Life' by Thomas Power

*ROI stands for Return on Investment

What is networking?

Do you think 'networking' is something to do with computers? It can be – it's connecting two or more computers together. Why do you want to connect them? So they can communicate with each other, back and forth, back and forth. Why do you want to do that? To achieve an objective, get a job done, earn some money.

It's exactly the same with business networking. It connects two or more people together so they can communicate back and forth, back and forth, achieve an objective, get a job done, and earn some money.

Now, how do you connect computers? Probably through some kind of cable. The strongest cable has multiple strands (it's broadband rather than dialup) and similarly, there are lots of networking channels you can choose from. And the more networking channels you have, the faster your connection:

- Formal or informal
- Social or business
- Online or offline
- Old boys' club or mums on the school run

It doesn't matter how or where you do it, my definition of networking is simply 'meeting people and making connections'. Other definitions include:

- Face-to-face marketing
- Word-of-mouth marketing
- Building relationships for long-term gain
- Finding and developing contacts for future work
- Farming not hunting

What are your networking objectives?

Before you decide whether to add networking to your marketing mix, you need to decide what you are trying to get out of it.

Here is an example checklist:

- Raise your profile .... ❏
- Boost your turnover............ ❏
- Launch new product .... ❏
- Find new clients................. ❏
- Source suppliers................. ❏
- Establish joint ventures .... ❏
- Acquire funding .... ❏
- Find a new job .... ❏
- Get promoted..................... ❏
- Learn something new .... ❏

What are **your** networking goals?

_____

_____

_____

It's best to write them down in a SMART format (Specific, Measurable, Attainable, Realistic, Time-bound) e.g.

I will attract 3 new customers through networking by the end of this year

OR

I will give referrals worth £xxx in the next six months

How does networking work?

It is said that you can reach anyone in the world in six steps or less. On a BBC2 documentary, researchers looked at this 'Six degrees of separation theory' and found that it works on a cellular level (in relation to disease) as well as on a global level (in relation to connectedness). They also found that it all falls apart without the 'hubs' – the well-connected people I've called 'networking tarts' (see page 50).

"I read somewhere that everybody on this planet is separated by only six other people. Six degrees of separation between us and everyone else on this planet. The President of the United States, a gondolier in Venice, just fill in the names. I find it A) extremely comforting that we're so close, and B) like Chinese water torture that we're so close because you have to find the right six people to make the right connection... I am bound to everyone on this planet by a trail of six people."
John Guare 'Six Degrees of Separation' (play 1990, film 1993)

The theory was tested with a trivia game called 'Six degrees of Kevin Bacon' (because he'd been in so many films he'd probably worked with everybody in Hollywood in six steps or less). At first, the actor was insulted (what's more, he turned out not to be the 'best-connected person in Hollywood' at all). Then, he turned it to his advantage. To find out more, search the story on Wikipedia, try it out on www.oracleofbacon.org and see www.sixdegrees. org, the charity that he established as a result.

Six degrees of separation

At one talk I gave, I tried an experiment to demonstrate the theory.

I asked people to stand up if they knew me before the meeting. About 12 people stood. Then I asked those who knew one of the people who was standing, to please stand up. I repeated this until no-one else stood up. When we looked around the room, almost everyone was standing. And, for those people who were still sitting, you can bet that someone in the room knew someone that they knew too.

Two degrees from the PM!

When I was asked if I could simplify Government information, I wondered how I might do that (if I ever wanted to). At a 'Spice Magic' networking event, I found that the organiser, Pinky Lilani, is also the founder of the Asian Women of Achievement Awards, with Cherie Blair as one of her patrons. At the end of the event, Pinky offered to pass on messages for attendees.

Also, my sister is a Pilates teacher who has worked with Stephanie who co-authored a book with Carol Caplin. Another route to the then-PM, Tony Blair!

Without even taking up these opportunities, I have since written copy for a Government website.

If we're in business, each of us probably knows at least 250 people. World champion networkers know hundreds more. The secret of networking is not to sell to the people you know (although that may happen), it's to tap into other people's networks.

It is said that 70% of business comes from word-of-mouth marketing. For me, nearly 100% of my business comes from people I know (or people who know me). So networking is an essential part of my marketing strategy.

If your business depends on who you are rather than on your brand name, then networking will work for you too. But only if you go about it the right way.

Networking DOs and DON'Ts

- Dress appropriately
- Arrive on time
- Trust serendipity about who you sit or stand beside
- Identify and introduce yourself to influencers e.g. speakers, organisers, champion networkers. If you can make a good impression on them, imagine who they could connect you to!
- Don't hard sell
- Don't give away your business card unless someone asks for it
- Collect business cards only if you actually plan to keep in touch
- Be friendly and nice
- Connect people
- If you promise to follow-up something with someone, do it promptly

Where can I go networking?

You can go out networking morning, noon and night if you want to! Here are just a few opportunities that I know of. Why not see if you can find a meeting near you?

- One-off events
    Exhibitions
    Seminars
    Conferences
    Workshops
- Regular events
    Chamber of Commerce
    Federation of Small Businesses (FSB)
    Rotary Club
    Round Table
    NetLinked
    Business Scene
- Weekly events
    Business Network International (BNI)
    Business Referral Exchange (BRX)
    Business Over Breakfast (BOB)
    Business For Breakfast (BFB)
    4Networking
    Venture Catalyst
- Women's lunch-time meetings
    1230 The Women's Company
    Sister Snog
- Hobby groups
- Speed networking
- Golf days

'It's not what you know, it's not even who you know...it's who knows you.'

You can't NOT network!

I was at a seminar during a really busy time. I thought to myself, "Right, that's it, I'm not networking today!" Nevertheless, the people sitting either side of me each said: "Hello, what do you do?" I told them, and they both asked for my card. Argh!

Feeding the pigeons

On Peter's sixth birthday, his father took him to the local park to feed the pigeons. Clutching a few slices of bread, Peter ran towards a group of pigeons. As he approached, all the pigeons flew away. The more he tried, the more pigeons left the park. His father put his arm around the little boy and said: 'Here, let me show you how it's done'.

His father broke off a few pieces of bread and began sprinkling them on the floor. After a while, a couple of curious pigeons began to peck cautiously at the bread. Gradually, they came a little closer. The father lowered his hand carefully, and opened his palm to display the crumbs. One pigeon eased forward and began to feed from his hand. Then another, followed by another and another.

If you want to develop great business referrals and business prospects then you need to make sure you do not scare people away by coming across as pushy. Be soft, and you will not scare off the very people that could connect you to your biggest ever piece of business.

Source: www.theaccidentalsalesman.com (edited)

How does breakfast networking work?

After informal networking, then breakfast and a few announcements, all the members present for one minute about who they are, what they do, why they are good at it, and most importantly, what they are looking for. Next, the guests get the same opportunity. Then, on a rota basis, one member gets to present for ten minutes so that over time you build up trust and understanding about who everybody is and what they do. It ends with a referral session where people pass their business contacts to each other. These are qualified leads where the potential client is already expecting your call because you have been personally recommended to them by the person who is giving the referral.

We are the champions!

At least one client has become a great champion of mine. He knows a lot of people and has referred a number of them to me. When I meet the potential clients I don't even have to do any 'selling' because he's already done it for me!

Which breakfast networking organisation should I choose?

BNI and BRX are the major options in the UK. To sum up the differences between the two, as I understand it, BNI started in the 1980s in America, it has hundreds of groups worldwide and in the UK, it has a tried and tested formula. BRX started in London in 1999 and has now spread as far as Scotland. It is a bit more relaxed, perhaps a bit more 'British' in its approach. As previously stated, there is also BOB, BFB and any number of others.

They all work, because networking works, no matter which organisation has arranged the meeting. My advice is to go along and try them all, because different styles suit different people. And then make your decision based on the people in the group rather than the organisation itself. Because if you are going to attend breakfast every week with the same people, it really needs to be a pleasure not a chore.

"Hello, what do you do?"

It's a typical (although boring) question, so you need to be prepared with an answer. Instead of saying: "I'm an accountant", why not say something customer-focused, such as:

I help my clients to avoid any problems with their tax returns and make sure their accounts are completed accurately and on time
I free up my clients to focus on their core business and enjoy their work, by taking away the worry of dealing with their tax returns and accounts
I help people get their taxes right so they don't pay a penny too much

If that's how NOT to start a conversation, then what should you say instead? Here are some ideas for easy opening lines:

Questions about the event
Have you been here before?
It's my first time at this event. Do you know the usual format?
I'm looking to meet ... Can you introduce me?
I enjoyed your talk and would love to find out more – can I treat you to lunch so I can ask your advice?
What did you think of the speaker?
Is there anyone you are particularly looking to meet?
How did you find out about this event?

Questions about work

How did you get into doing what you do?

How has your industry changed since you first started work?

What are you working on at the moment?

Are you keeping busy?

How are you coping with the recession?

What is your favourite type of client?

How do new clients find about about you?

What is the one piece of advice you would give your clients?

What's been the highlight of the past year for you?

What are your plans for the next year?

What did you dream of doing when you were younger?

Is there anything else you'd like to do (other than what you are doing now)?

What are you doing differently now compared with five years ago?

General questions

I've been admiring your jacket / tie / haircut. Where did you get it?

What do you like to do outside work?

Have you had a holiday so far this year?

Did you see ... on TV last night?

What football team do you support?

Have you read any good books lately?

What was your most embarrassing moment?

What is the funniest thing that has ever happened to you?

If you were hosting a dinner party with anybody living or dead, who would you invite?

What is your proudest achievement?

Questioning techniques

If you ask 'closed' questions, you will only get a one-word yes/no answer. Your aim is to start a conversation, so ask 'open' questions. They usually start with WWWWWH – who, what, when, where, why or how.

Exercise

Write an 'open' opening question you would be happy to use:

_____

_____

_____

Note that it's OK to talk about subjects that are not business-related. In fact, it's a good idea! In the same way that you would often start a client meeting with some general chit-chat about the weather, your journey or whatever was going on in your life, you can start a networking conversation on any subject you like, and go on to talk about business afterwards.

Andy Lopata tells how the conversation was drying up at a networking dinner he attended, until he started talking about football. The event took a much more lively turn, everyone enjoyed it more, and better quality relationships were built.

Top tip: Salesmen tend to make the worst networkers. In accordance with their training, they are always trying to 'close the deal' instead of trying to build relationships.

How should I network effectively?

We've looked at what networking is and where to do it, but how do you do it and do it well?

Here are my own personal top ten tips:

1. Have a good product or service to offer
You have to be clear about what you are selling, and you have to be enthusiastic about it. If you can't wake up excited on a Monday morning you're doing the wrong job. Life's too short for that.

2. Talk about the benefits not the features
Take the customer's point of view. Don't say 'Here's what I'm offering, why not buy it'. Talk about how you can save people money, or time or hassle, about what problems you can solve. Sum it up in one sentence. I'm not talking about a mission statement. I'm talking about a simple sentence in Plain English.

3. Don't sell
People buy from people, so just be friendly and nice and when people know what you do they will want to do business with you. We all know what it's like when someone tries to sell to us. We know they are after the money in our pocket and we don't want to give it to them!

Networking is so easy, just turn up on time, be professional, do what you say you will do, and smile! That's the type of person that everybody likes to work with.

World's Worst Networker

Ironically, I met him at an event where networking guru, Andy Lopata, had just given a speech about 'how not to network'. Andy suggested that you never use the opening question: "What do you do?" Instead, you start a conversation about something that you might have in common, such as the weather, or the traffic, or how you both came to be at the same event. That way, you start to build relationships, not attempt to 'sell' in a room full of people who are not ready to 'buy'.

Shortly after Andy shared these words of wisdom, I was having a lovely chat with two new people when a third stranger burst in.

"Hope you don't mind me interrupting you?" he asked.

Hmm, well, yes, it did seem a bit rude.

He thrust a yellow leaflet into each of our hands.

"Let me tell you what I do," he continued, and went on to explain.

I felt like shredding his yellow leaflet and throwing it back at him.

"Didn't you hear the speech?" I asked him (while my new friends fell about laughing).

He looked at me blankly. Then turned away to interrupt the group that was standing beside us.

The saddest part is, when I read his leaflet, I found the World's Worst Networker offers a service that I might actually like to buy or recommend to my friends.

But now, simply because of his boorish behaviour, I have no intention of doing so.

Sadly, there are still a few people who behave like that at networking events, trying to 'sell'. Trouble is, most people are not there to buy, so why try selling to them? And if you're not there to sell, then what do you do?

"Hello, hello, hello"

Remember I told you the secret of successful networking is just to be friendly and nice? Yet in my first-ever appraisal at my first-ever job, I was told off for being unfriendly. "Why do people think I'm unfriendly?" I asked. "Because you never say hello to them when you pass them in the corridor," I was told. "That's because I'm short-sighted," I replied, "and I just can't see them properly!" I soon got new glasses and made friends with everyone. My next appraisal was much more complimentary!

Top tip: Always act pleased to meet people – there's no excuse not to!

Smile please!

In my old job there was one HR officer who always used to act as though she was delighted I'd walked into her office. Giving me a huge smile, she'd exclaim: "Jaaackie! Hello!" It became a joy to visit her and it taught me some valuable lessons.

- People like you if you behave as though you like them
- People enjoy the company of people who appear to be enjoying themselves
- Smiling makes you feel good
- It takes more muscles to frown than to smile
- Smiling on the phone changes your vocal tone and generates a better response

4. Listen

Don't do all the talking. Ask questions instead. Everyone has something interesting about them, whether it's the job they do, or a hobby that they are passionate about. And people love to be asked for advice. So if you see someone that you admire, go and ask how they achieved their success. Or even ask someone where they got their lovely jacket, just to start a conversation.

5. Be helpful

Make connections for people. I now know so many people I feel like Cilla Black on Blind Date! I listen to what people say, I know who they need to speak to and then I put them together. After that, I leave them to it. They don't always tell me what happens next – I haven't yet had to buy a hat but you never know!

The BNI slogan of 'Givers Gain' applies here. Like anything, the more you put in, the more you get out. All you need to do is connect the relevant people to each other and sooner or later someone will return the favour to you.

6. Prepare and follow-up

When you attend an event, don't just count the time you are at the event and travel time, also include the time it takes to prepare what you are going to say, who you are looking to meet and what questions you might ask. And afterwards, follow it up with a message to say 'Nice to meet you' and perhaps refer to something you learned. If you have offered to connect someone, make sure you act on it as quickly as possible. Do it the very next day if you can. Invite them to sign up to your newsletter (if you haven't already) so you can keep in touch by offering them valued advice, hints or humour. Remember that meeting new people is just the start. Keeping in touch or booking a one-to-one with them helps you get to know each other better.

7. Accept every invitation

There are lots of networking opportunities out there and my advice is, just try them all (within reason), until you find which suits you best.

8. Repetition. Repetition. Repetition.

Once you've found an event you like, keep going back. Unless it was sooooo deadly boring that you just couldn't stand it! But if you thought there was a kernel, a nugget, the merest hint of something worthwhile that might turn into an opportunity, then you have to keep going back.

Let's face it, it's unlikely that you will meet someone on day one who says: "Hoorah, you provide exactly what I want, let me give you all the money in my pocket!" It can take 6 to 8 meetings before someone turns from a stranger into a customer. That's why weekly breakfasts work so well, it can be only 6 to 8 weeks before you get some business. But if you go to a monthly event, it takes 6 to 8 months. With bi-monthly events, it can take a couple of years.

9. ASK for what you want

Don't try to sell to the person standing in front of you, ask who they know that you could help. This is where the BRX slogan applies, of 'who do you know who'. Be specific. If you save people money, then don't ask: 'Who do you know that wants to save money'. The answer to that is 'everybody', it's too general. Instead ask: 'Who do you know that's a single parent, or an OAP, or a student, or struggling for cash at the moment'. That might lead you to a specific person or piece of business.

Top tip: Never underestimate anybody – the next person you talk to might be related to your dream client, they might play golf together or live next door. Everyone has a story to tell. It's your job to chat to them and be open to anything until you discover it.

Superstar

My stationery supplier invited me to a gig he was doing at the local live music venue. I thought I'd just go along to support him. It turned out he was lead vocalist for a soul/funk band that were huge in the '80s – they were still touring and recording with some of the world's most famous artists. They gave a fabulous performance and it was a tip-top night out!

You never know...

I was invited to run a mini-workshop for a women's networking group in Sevenoaks, to help members improve their marketing skills. I'd expected about 40 people to be in the audience. Hoorah, lots of people to expose my business to! However, only 12 turned up. "Oh well," I thought, "I'm a professional, I can still deliver an hour of information-packed training in a fun way!"

You just never know who you're going to meet.

It turned out that one of the attendees was the director of a training company that runs more open courses in Kent than any other local organisation. And she was looking for a new marketing trainer!

I'm proud to say she invited me to join them as an Associate, and they went on to book me to run a range of courses for them.

10. Be confident

Don't shuffle around and be shy and modest about what you do. The more confident you appear, the more opportunities you will attract.

And here's the secret to appearing confident. Just pretend. All you have to do is **pretend**. Because, honestly, nobody except you knows the difference.

There was some research about people's biggest fears. Death came third! The number one fear was walking into a room full of strangers, and number two was speaking in public. Yet that's exactly what you have to do when you go out networking. So we're all just as nervous as each other!

Pretending

I remember the first time I went to Toastmasters (the public speaking organisation). David welcomed me at the door, I shook his hand and took a seat in the front row, not knowing that's where all the dignatories usually sit. The second time, I took a safe seat in the back row. In the warm-up, people had to say the thing that had most impressed them about the person beside them. It happened that I was sitting next to David, and he said that he was most impressed by my confidence the first time I'd visited the group.

'Confidence, what confidence?' I thought.

You see, what I felt the first time was: 'Oh my God, I've never been here before, I don't know what's going to happen, I don't know anyone, look at all these people, what if I have to stand up and speak or do something embarrassing?'

You see, inside this confident exterior is a trembling worm of shyness.

But I learned a secret – let me share it with you now.

Some years ago when I was a junior manager in a large organisation, I undertook some training in presentation skills. I was incredibly shy. One of the first exercises was to ask another delegate for a lift home in the style of the organiser's choosing. The styles were listed on a flipchart. I just didn't want to do it, and left my turn until last. By then, the only word left was 'seductive'. I really, really didn't want to do it! I was either going to run crying to the toilet or I'd just have to do what they wanted.

I took a deep breath, and here's what I did.

I draped myself 'seductively' over the table in front of one of the male delegates and walked my fingers teasingly towards him as I slowly said: "Hello... You know this course we're on is called... 'Dynamic'... Presentations?" He nodded. "Well... why don't you give me lift home and we'll see just how... dynamic... we can be!"

Everybody laughed!

How gratifying. It was a break-through for me.

By the end of the course we were asked to present something about one of our hobbies. Mine was jazz dancing, so I opened the presentation with a little dance routine and a 'ta da!' dramatic flourish!

What I'd gained was the **permission** to do anything I wanted, and the **courage** to fake it.

Top tip: If you can do Charades with the family at home at Christmas, you can 'act' anywhere.

How do I 'work the room'?

When you walk into a room full of people, you might naturally gravitate towards someone you recognise. Of course, it's fine to say hello to them, but networking involves taking a chance and meeting somebody new. Go on, break out of your comfort zone! Just tell your friend: 'Lovely to catch up with you, but now, let's mingle' or: 'Time to get another drink!'

One Two Three
If you see someone standing on their own, they will be most grateful when you go and talk to them. They haven't gone networking to be on their own!

If you see two people in deep conversation, it's best not to interrupt. They might be on the point of doing an important deal.

If you see three people (or a group) it's easier to join in. Stand beside them, listen to the conversation, nod when you agree with something, and – as soon as there is an opening – introduce yourself, ask a question or participate in the discussion.

The networking handshake
The most common form of business greeting is the handshake, yet many people don't seem to do it right! There is a comfortable mid-point between loosely taking the tip of someone's fingers (which feels like holding a wet fish), and gripping their knuckles tightly (which feels as though your hand is being crushed). These days, men shouldn't kiss a woman's hand (it comes across as outdated and smarmy) nor tickle their palm (that's just creepy). The secret is the web-to-web grip. Look at the 'web' between your thumb and index finger. The perfect handshake is when the web on your hand meets the web on the other person's hand.

Eye contact

Obviously, it's not polite to look around the room while you're talking to someone, in the hope of finding someone more interesting to talk to. The person that is talking can look away briefly while they speak; it gives them a chance to think. However, the person that is listening should maintain eye contact with the person that is speaking, to show they are paying attention.

Personal space

Some people are more touchy-feely than others, and you have to be careful in a business context. You know how uncomfortable it feels when someone stands too close to you? Similarly, another person will get twitchy if you stand too close to them.

(((Hugz)))

A male colleague once complained to me about a female associate who used to hug him every time they met at the coffee machine. He knew she was just being friendly, but told me he felt 'physically assaulted' every time she said hello.

Body language

To build rapport, you can match or mirror the actions, pace of speaking and even the breathing of the person you are talking to. Note that folded arms can mean 'closed' and uninterested, while feet are a dead giveaway! When standing, if someone's feet are pointing away from you (especially if they point towards the door), it means they probably want to escape! People wagging their feet while seated, could be bored or angry. And the angle of someone's feet even shows when they fancy you!

Booze

At evening networking events, alcohol is sometimes served. That's fine, but take care not to overdo it. You still need to behave professionally (true, you might meet someone you find particularly – let's say – interesting, but it's best to save the flirting for a more social occasion!).

Cheers?

At one event, a man reeking of red wine came up behind me and leered over my shoulder, making inappropriate remarks. It was deeply unpleasant. I couldn't be bothered to confront him, and chose to leave the event early instead.

At another, a lonely old soul got chatting to me about pensions. Despite my best efforts, he had no other conversational topics to offer. No-one else was polite enough to talk to him at all, so he followed me around all evening. He even waited for me outside the ladies' loo! That was another occasion when I left before the end of the event. Fortunately, he didn't follow me home.

Business card etiquette

In the UK, it's OK to make notes on the back of a business card. It helps you remember specific things about the person or what you've promised them, when you follow-up afterwards (you **do** follow-up your networking contacts, don't you?). The thicker the card, the better quality the brand appears.

Top tip: To be perceived as professional, do not use free business cards e.g. Vistaprint. If you must, then at least pay the extra to get their logo taken off the back.

It's important to respect cultural differences. For instance, in Japan, it's polite to hand over your card with two hands. And **never** be seen to write on a Japanese business card; they have to be treated with respect! The thinner the card, the more important the person. If the business card is like tissue paper, you're probably talking to the Biggest of all Big Bosses!

Top tip: Don't waste space on the back of your business card. You can use it for selling messages, a testimonial or bullet points (something that shows the benefit of your product or service to your customers).

Male v female networking

I've heard it said that women don't need to be taught how to network. It just comes naturally to us. It's true that we are used to passing on recommendations – imagine mums on the school run referring a good painter/decorator to each other, for example. For women, its all about collaboration, not competition (I realise this is a sweeping generalisation, of course).

Men sometimes come at networking with a more competitive attitude. They are less used to 'giving' in order to 'receive' (ooer, missus). What's more, in conversation, they are more used to interrupting or talking over people, and less used to adding the "Really?", "That's interesting" and "Mmm, tell me more" type of phrases, that women often use to help conversations flow.

Top tip: As a woman in a predominantly male business environment, it's easier to stand out and get noticed in the crowd – just wear a brightly coloured outfit instead of a black or grey suit (this can boost your confidence too).

"Hello, Wossname!"

Back in the '80s, I did some copywriting for Jeff Banks, when
he was at Warehouse. We met at his studio in Angel, Islington,
to discuss the brief (it was about describing the detail on black
trousers that had been photographed against a black background).
I remember noting his manicured fingernails and the fact that
he seemed addicted to Extra Strong Mints! A week or two later,
I was back at his studio, to see the clothes on rails and write the
copy. He didn't know I would be there that day, but spotted me
from the other side of the room and came over to say hello. I
was extremely impressed that he remembered my name. Him, a
famous fashion designer! Me, a lowly copywriter!

Help, I can't remember names!

It's good practice, when you go out networking, to remember the
names of the people you've been introduced to. But it isn't always
easy. Names are stored in a different bit of your brain to other
words so they are harder to recall.

When you meet someone you are definitely interested in, maybe
because they are important from a work point of view, or you find
them particularly fanciable, there's no way you'd ever forget what
they're called. You remember their name without even trying. But
what do you do when you meet people, perhaps several at once,
and you're not sure of their importance to you, or whether you'll
ever meet them again?

If you're a highly visual person, then visualise their name in
as complex and detailed a way as possible to 'code' it more
effectively in your memory bank. If you are more auditory, try

repeating their name back to them. And if you're really stuck, just apologise for forgetting and ask them again what their name is!

Mental images

I was at a networking dinner with some new people plus one I knew well, and one I'd only ever emailed. Of course it was easy for me to remember the name of my friend, and easy to 'put a face to the name' of the person I'd exchanged emails with. Within a few moments, I met the others.

Paul was going a bit bald. Paul and 'bald' sound similar. That got his name stored. Mike and Mark, ooer, might be easy to muddle those two! Mike was tall, and wearing a long tie. Tie. Looking and sounding like the letter I. I as in Mike. Mark had a moustache, like a smudgy mark (Mark) under his nose. Easy, that got those two sorted. Yasmin had on a black waistcoat with a white shirt underneath. The shape of the neckline made a Y, and that helped me 'fix' her name in my mind. Chantal was wearing a striking choker necklace, turned sideways it looked like the letter C. That helped me to 'log' her name too.

This technique worked for that evening. But what if, next time you meet the same people, they are wearing different clothes?

When you expect to meet people again, you can add 'imaginary' visuals. Picture Paul in a tug'o'war ("puuuull!"), Mike singing karaoke (mike = microphone), Mark doing graffiti ('marking' the wall), Yasmin with Simon le Bon (he's married to model Yasmin Parvaneh), Chantal drinking Champagne (similar sounding French words). The stronger the mental image you create, the better your memory for names will be.

Running your own weekly networking meetings: recipe for success

Ingredients

- Display materials such as signage, posters or banners
- Invitations, sent by post or email
- Name badges for attendees
- Dynamic chairman
- Well-delegated committee of eager volunteers
- Regular members, shapes and sizes not important (every member is an essential ingredient, but on days when a particular individual can't attend, they should be substituted by someone else)
- Visitors

Preparation

Find a good venue with nice, helpful staff. It must be conveniently located for local business people to reach, and have all the usual facilities, such as plenty of parking. It may also serve tasty refreshments at a reasonable price.

Gently blend chairman with committee, to ensure all tasks are undertaken by people with the right levels of commitment and ability.

Mix in a constant stream of guests to keep the group alive. Potential visitors are all around even though some people may think they're as rare as truffles. Offer incentives as a reward and 'thank you' to anyone who brings a guest that joins.

Top tip: New members are at their most enthusiastic; they've just made a commitment to join and will be likely to justify their rationale to others. You can build on this by encouraging new members to bring guests along.

Method

On the day, use your display materials to 'brand' the room – people need to know they are attending a professional event.

Set up a 'reception desk', recording attendance and issuing name badges so everyone knows who is whom.

Top tip: Wear name badges on the right-hand side so they are in the natural line of sight when people shake hands.

Nominate a few smiley visitor hosts to seek out and welcome guests. The hosts should tell each guest what they can expect from the meeting, introduce them to anyone who may be of interest, and make sure they enjoy the event.

Top tip: Remember to follow-up all visitors by asking for feedback to guide your group's growth, and offering an invitation to join if they fit the group's criteria.

Throw in a series of entertaining, informative and enlightening presentations so attendees get added value (optional).

Sprinkle with a big dose of humour.

Add a number of quality referrals and leave to simmer.

Before serving, top with a handful of serial networkers (a.k.a. 'networking tarts') as they are the greatest givers, have the widest networks, can make more connections, and bring the most referrals to the meeting. If you can impress them and persuade them to join, they also get the most out of their membership.

Top tip: You'll probably find them out networking!

Cook at room temperature until done.

Exercise

Prepare a one-minute speech that includes:

- Who you are
- What you do
- Why you're good at it
- What you're looking for

_____
_____
_____
_____
_____
_____
_____
_____
_____
_____
_____

Speed Networking

Inspired by speed dating, this is a 'quantity not quality' approach to networking. In my experience, you could easily get bored with the sound of your own voice repeating your carefully honed one-minute script (you do have one prepared, don't you?). And you can barely remember who's who with all the business cards you've collected. The secret to success is the follow-up. Contact all the people you've met, and arrange one-to-ones with them (if appropriate).

Top tip: If it's a 'standing' event, wear comfy shoes!

Meeting competitors

One of the people I met at a speed networking event was a copywriter, like myself. There was absolutely no point in us 'pitching' to each other for business, so we just had a lovely chat about the kind of work we each liked doing and 'clients from hell'. Afterwards, I forgot all about it.

Then I 'met' her again on Ecademy (online networking). We chatted and got to know each other a bit better. Instead of being competitors, we ended up as friends and associates. From time to time, we meet for lunch and a girly chat.

One day when she was overloaded with work, she passed it on to me. Another day, the same happened to me, and I passed the work on to her. Next time, I was too busy to take on her extra work myself, and passed it on to another copywriter we both knew. I asked her why she hadn't passed it on to him direct. She explained: "Because when I first met you, you were friendly and nice. When I met him, he treated me like a competitor."

Top tip: Competitors can be your best source of referrals, so turn them into collaborators instead.

Why does networking need such a regular commitment?

When I worked in the home shopping world, we used to segment our customer database by Recency, Frequency and Value. Those people who ordered most recently, most frequently or with the highest value were more likely to order again. I believe the same principles apply to networking.

If someone asks you, "Do you know a good yoga teacher?" Are you going to remember the one you met last week or the one you met last year?

Obviously, it's the one you met most recently.

And if they ask, "Do you know a good electrician?" Are you going to remember the one you met just once or the one you have met 6 or 8 times or more?

You will first think of the one you meet most frequently.

And if they ask, "Do you know a good Independent Financial Advisor?" Are you going to remember the one who has done nothing for you or the one who has generated your goodwill by giving advice and support and perhaps by passing referrals to you in the past?

You'll recommend the one who has most value to you.

The lesson is clear. You want to be in the front of the minds of your networking colleagues, so if they fall into conversation anytime about your product or service, they can recommend you.

With weekly networking, all aspects of Recency, Frequency and Value are working for you. You are never more than seven days away from seeing each other, you meet up to 48 times a year, and you gain value by contributing over time.

It's rare to meet someone on day one who says, "Great, you offer exactly what I need, let me give you some money!" As previously mentioned, this can happen, but more often it takes at least 6 to 8 interactions for a stranger to achieve enough trust and understanding to place an order with you.

So, with weekly networking meetings, you can start expecting results within two or three months of joining. With monthly or bi-monthly meetings, it takes a lot longer to build those trusted relationships.

How do I get best results from networking?

As you read this section, think about where you are on this 'networking ladder', and more importantly, where you want to be.

Me Me Me
Most people join networking organisations to get business for themselves. They are in it for Me Me Me. Fair enough. That's how most of us started.

Team spirit
It took me a year to realise that's not how it works. Maybe I'm a bit slow, but it took me a whole year to learn how to carry the rest of my group members 'in the back of my head' between meetings, so that when I fall into conversation about mortgages, for example, I can recommend my mortgage broker team-mate from the group.

Network the network

Having had that lightbulb moment, it didn't take me long to move up to the next level. When you join BRX you don't just join one group, but a whole network with groups right across the UK. If your discipline doesn't clash with existing members, you can present your business at any group. Offer to substitute for an absent member and you even get your breakfast free, while extending your own network and seeing how another group functions.

Networking tart!

These are the people who belong to more than one networking organisation and accept just about every invitation they receive. Instead of knowing about 250 people, as average business owners do, they know 1,000 people or more.

So who do you think gives and gets the most referrals? Well, it's not the Me Me Me people, that's for sure. When you're a Networking Tart, giving and getting referrals is easy! You become known as a hub of useful contacts, so people come to you to ask "Do you know a good accountant" and you can say "Hey, I know a great accountant, would you like his contact details?"

Like anything, the more you put in, the more you get out. So if you give referrals to people in the group, people will give referrals to you. It's the way the universe works!

A networking tart accepts every invitation they receive (within reason). There are loads of networking opportunities out there, I recommend you try them all until you find which suits you best.

Just dive in

I shopped around four different breakfast groups before I found the one I joined. I chose them because they were talking about scuba diving, not business. "Aha!" I thought. "This is where I fit in! Meeting these people every week will be a pleasure not a chore!"

Top tip: A successful networking event works because of the people in the group, not because of the organisation that runs it. Keep visiting until you find a group with a dynamic leadership team, plenty of active members, a good environment, a constant stream of new guests.

Zero cost marketing

When I started Comms Plus, I used all the usual marketing tools - advertising, direct mail, telemarketing etc. But now my marketing budget is down to zero. Nil. Nothing. Because 98% of my work comes from people I know, repeat business and referrals.

How do I do this? Through word-of-mouth marketing, also known as networking. So it's a strategic essential for me to get to know a lot of people. Or rather, for a lot of people to get to know me. In fact I became the Networking Queen of my local area! A complete Networking Tart! Because, for four or five years, I went to nearly every event I was invited to.

I networked hard for years, sometimes attending four events per week. Now, I don't need to network so hard any more, and just visit events as the speaker, a guest or a substitute for an absent member. I go because it's fun, I enjoy it, I reconnect with people I know and meet new ones. I don't go because I need the business. And, because I'm not desperate, I win business anyway.

How should I present myself?

People trust authority figures. Job title (e.g. Executive), trappings (e.g. posh car) and clothing (e.g. corporate suit) all play a part. If you are perceived as an authority figure, people will take you more seriously and be more willing to pay you money.

"Merely following orders"

Yale University psychologist, Stanley Milgram, famously conducted a series of experiments in the 1960s, to study obedience to authority, even when in conflict with moral values. A subject 'teacher' was tasked by the experimenter (the authority figure) to give an electric shock of increasing voltage to a 'learner' each time they got an answer wrong. In reality, there were no shocks. The learners were actors, briefed to bang on the dividing wall, scream with pain and eventually fall silent. Although many subjects wanted to stop the experiment and check on the learner, most continued after being prompted to proceed and assured by the experimenter that they would not be held responsible.

Before conducting the experiment, poll respondents believed that only a few (average 3%) would be prepared to inflict the maximum voltage. However, in Milgram's first set of experiments, 65% of participants administered the final massive 450-volt 'shock', though many were very uncomfortable doing so.

Present yourself as an authority

Look, act and dress the part. To build your confidence, you can enhance your individual style with colour, work on your presentation skills, and behave as though you are already the success you deserve to be.

Dress for success

When I was a junior employee, I was advised to dress 'one level up' in order to get the promotion I craved. Smart, instead of smart casual. I started wearing corporate suits instead of jeans. I also started answering the phone with my own name (as if people were phoning to speak to ME) rather than answering it with the name of the department.

When I was eventually promoted, a number of people told me, "Oh, I thought you were already a Senior Manager".

What can I say in my one-minute?

At many networking meetings, you are given the opportunity to give a 60-second 'elevator pitch' – imagine you are in a lift with Bill Gates (or your ideal client) and only have one minute to tell them about your business. It's like a walking, talking advert.

People often ask me to help with their one-minute speeches. There are endless permutations for things to say, but the objective is always to trigger more referrals.

General

Remember you are briefing your 'sales team' to go out and find you suitable referrals each week - you are not asking for business from the people in the room (although that may happen as a by-product). That's why BRX recommend the phrase 'Who do you know who...'

Structure

Top and tail your presentation with the same information each week, and vary the middle bit (the filling in the sandwich). Start with your name and company name and perhaps a 'tease' that gets attention. At the end, repeat your name and company name, with your catchphrase or slogan as a memory hook.

Catchphrase

I met the late Sir John Harvey-Jones at a networking event at Australia House. He was mingling with the crowd before his talk, and asking people: 'And what is it that you do?' He reached the little cluster where I was standing. The first guy answered: 'I'm in IT.' Sir John made a polite reply. The second guy answered: 'I'm an accountant.' Sir John said something equally dull. Then he asked me.

'I do Writing Without Waffle,' I said, pleased to have a catchy strapline that always prompts a good response.

He laughed, relieved at having something meatier to discuss. 'Oh, do you think you could do that for the Government?'

'I don't think there are enough hours in the day!' I said, and we went on to have a lovely conversation.

Be creative

I'll always remember one presentation given by the graphic designer in my BRX group. He stood up with his notes in his hand...and said nothing. He looked at his notes. He looked at us. He smiled...and still said nothing. He looked at his watch, looked at us...and still said nothing. After 30 seconds, he started to speak (half-a-minute of silence feels like a very long time!). "See how uncomfortable you feel when you don't hear from somebody? That's how your clients feel when you don't keep in touch with them.' He went on to promote his newsletter design service.

A BNI networking friend told me about another graphic designer, who shared this story in their 60-second presentation: "A beggar played the violin for two hours in the subway, and earned $30. The night before, that same violinist played in a concert hall to 2,000 people who'd each paid $100 per ticket. The performer played the same instrument (a $200,000 violin). He played the same tunes. The one thing that made such a difference to the amount he earned, was his branding."

Exercise

What can **you** say or do in your one-minute pitch, to make your presentation stand out from the rest?

_____
_____
_____
_____
_____

Enjoy

Make sure your product or service is something that you enjoy. If you have a passion for what you do, your enthusiasm will infect the people around you.

Your ideal client

I find that many networkers are very good at describing what they do, but are not so good at asking for what they want. OK, all of us want clients that have big budgets, pay on time and don't mess us around! But requesting those clients doesn't make it easy for the people in the room to find you a referral. Instead, why not take one industry in turn from your existing client list, and ask for referrals to more of the same?

Synergies

You can also ask for referrals to people in the same industry as yourself - for example, as a copywriter it is always useful for me to meet other writers, graphic designers, web designers, printers, photographers, and others in the creative industry. Not because they will become clients of mine, but because we might have potential clients in common; I could add value to their service offering, and they could add value to mine.

So who do you know that would be useful to have in your own network?

Be specific

Facilities Manager, Steve Turner, was at a training session in Croydon, and he asked "Who do you know that works in the Canon building in Wallington?" He knew they had an ugly old air conditioning system hanging out of their windows, and he knew he could offer them a better one. Someone in the room put up their hand, they had worked in that building for 15 years and still knew people there! The referral was made.

But do you think it would have worked if Steve had said 'Who do you know that needs new air conditioning?' or 'Who do you know that needs a facilities manager?'

I know it's tempting to cover everything you do at every meeting, but if you ask for something specific, and change it every week, just see how the referrals roll in!

Trust and understanding
Testimonials and case studies sell you more powerfully than anything you can say about yourself. People love stories about people. So use your one-minute to talk about what problem you solved for your client that week, what the solution was and what results you achieved for them. This technique gives the other members the confidence to refer you.

Be seen as an expert
How about sharing a weekly 'handy hint'? People learn something useful, it demonstrates your expertise and generates enormous amounts of goodwill e.g. the free tips booklets on my website!

Show don't tell
A picture tells a thousand words! So, if you have a product, then bring it along. Use a prop to demonstrate your service. Bring examples of work you have completed. This makes your presentation stand out from the rest, and visually demonstrates what you do.

There was an IT expert who presented a red lacy bra and a can of oil and said, "We provide support and maintenance!"
Source: Andy Lopata

When you write a novel, you are advised to 'show not tell'. You don't write 'He was angry'. Instead you write a scene when he comes into the room, shouting and throwing things around. The same applies to your networking speeches.

At her first-ever networking event, an image consultant had the chance to present to an audience of about 200 women. She'd prepared her speech and noted key words on index cards as a prompt. When she got on stage, she was so nervous she dropped all the cards on the floor and resorted to demonstrating what she does rather than talking about it. She called three people onto the stage, one brunette, one blonde and one redhead, and draped a different-coloured scarf around each of their necks. The whole audience went: "Ooh, that's not right!" She swapped the scarves around and the whole audience responded: "Ah, that's better!" After the session, there was a queue of people waiting to get her business card.
Source: Philip Calvert, Professional Speaker

Make 'em laugh
People do business with people they like. And people like people who do serious business in a light-hearted way. It's OK to add appropriate humour to your networking presentations and conversations. People will enjoy your company more, and look forward to dealing with you.

Standing out in a crowd

At a networking meeting with over 100 attendees, everyone had just 30 seconds to make their 'pitch'. One guy stood on a chair, and told us his sales training business was 'head and shoulders above the rest.' He certainly got himself noticed!

Unusual suspects

In most networking groups, you get an accountant, solicitor and IFA/mortgage broker. You'll probably find an IT expert, graphic/web designer and photographer too. In some groups, you get a cluster of tradespeople: plumber, electrician and painter/decorator. You may also meet some alternative therapists, such as masseur, hypnotherapist and reflexologist.

However, one networking breakfast I was at included three of the most unusual guests I've ever met. It was early on a Friday morning, and the experience was so surreal I thought I was still dreaming!

The first guest stood up and said: "Hello. Who do you know that has a heart?" It turned out he was one of the most eminent heart surgeons in the UK.

The second guest stood up and said: "Hello, I'm in security." I thought he was another alarm salesman, but no. He did Close Protection (bodyguarding) for celebrities and VIPs visiting danger zones such as Iraq.

The third guest was wearing a tight black T-shirt with diamanté trim. She looked dressed to go to a nightclub rather than a business meeting. She stood up and said: "Hello, I used to be a prostitute. I now supply attractive people to lie on your dinner table at parties covered with food. Your guests then eat off their naked bodies without using their hands."

You don't usually meet this sort of people out networking. And, funnily enough, none of them signed up for membership!

Cheers!

I attended a meeting where I didn't know anybody. In my one-minute presentation, I told the story of Threshers' Christmas offer – they emailed their suppliers with a link to a 40% discount voucher off their wine and Champagne. Probably seemed like a good idea at the time. But they didn't realise that the suppliers would pass the link on to all their friends. The Threshers website crashed with the number of hits it got, and it was estimated that half-a-million vouchers were printed.

Everyone laughed when I explained that all Threshers needed was an experienced copywriter to add the words 'limited offer' so they could restrict take-up and avoid losing so much money.

It might have been a deliberate strategy on Threshers' part because they got more column inches of media coverage about the campaign going 'wrong'. But the story worked for me. When I stood up again for the referrals session, everyone was already smiling in anticipation of what I would say.

The truth is, no-one buys from you because of what you say in your one-minute. They buy from you because of what you say and how you behave **in between** your one-minutes. The chat you have about football. The favour you do them when you introduce them to one of your contacts. Or the worthwhile contribution you make to the committee so the meetings run smoothly.

How do I GET referrals?

The secret of getting referrals is to:

- Be friendly and nice so people like you
- Do a good job so clients recommend you
- Always turn up when you say you will so people trust that you won't let them (or their contacts) down
- Present yourself professionally so your confidence in yourself increases other people's confidence in you
- Make a contribution to the group (whether it's by giving referrals, or joining the committee, or being the life-and-soul of every party) – as with anything, the more you put in, the more you get out
- Be memorable to impress people you meet, especially any influencers who are extremely well connected (yes, the 'networking tarts'!)
- Communicate clearly so people know the kind of referrals you're looking for and how they can help
- Have a unique marketing message to stand out from your competitors (such as a catchy slogan summarising your USP)

People have to **understand** what you do and the referrals you are looking for, **trust** that you will deliver on your promises, and **like** you well enough to want to refer you.

To build understanding, be simple and clear in your one-minute presentation. To build trust, always behave professionally and do what you say you will. To build liking, just be friendly and nice!

How do I GIVE referrals?

Some people are concerned about this, especially if they don't meet many people during the course of their work. Don't panic, you are not expected to do business with other people in your group yourself (unless you want to).

To give referrals, you have to learn the trick of keeping your contacts in the front of your mind all the time, so that whenever a conversation arises where it's appropriate to recommend them, you can make the introduction on their behalf. You need to change your mindset from 'me, me, me' and recognise that you are part of a team, a group, a network. Your networking colleagues become friends, and we all refer our friends the same way our friends would refer us.

Remember, you may **like** someone well enough, but if you know they are untrustworthy, you're never going to refer them. If you **trust** them, but don't understand exactly what they are looking for, you probably can't help them. If you **understand** what they do and what they want, but don't actually like them very much, you are unlikely to recommend them to your valued contacts.

Despite what you might think, you probably know at least 250 people. Your aim is to connect these contacts with any members of your group where you identify a suitable opportunity. You don't have to recommend any fellow networker unless you really do trust they will give good service. You don't have to put forward your valuable contacts to your colleagues in the group, unless you genuinely believe that networker could benefit them – it's your reputation that's at stake. When you are connecting people, you can explain how well you know them. For example: "I met Felicity last month. I've never worked with her myself but I have heard very good things about her service." Or: "I've known James for four years. He's done some work in my own house and in my neighbour's house, and I trust him completely."

Exercise

Write the name of someone you know in at least five of these categories:

- Family _____
- Friend_____
- Supplier _____
- Colleague _____
- Client_____
- Neighbour_____
- Club / Church / Hobby _____

See, there's at least five already! Someone you know might like to be introduced to any of these people.

Top tip: Go to other networking groups and you'll soon meet more people.

Join the 5cm high club

After 5 years of active networking I had a pile of referral slips about 5cm high. They represent every referral I've given over the years. I don't suppose for one minute that all of those have turned into business (although they were all given with genuine good intention). And I must admit I haven't received anything like that number of referrals in return (but I have received plenty of referral business to make it all worthwhile).

The truth is that not all referrals work out well. I've given out referrals that I know have not been followed up for whatever reason. And I've responded to referrals I've received and found that the contact was not really interested in talking to me after all.

And, a couple of times, I've passed referrals on that didn't work out at all.

When referrals go horribly wrong

I introduced an IFA to one of my relatives, for inheritance tax planning. The IFA was supposedly an expert in this area, and of course it could have been in my best interests for the relationship to work out! I don't know exactly what happened, but my relative ended up throwing the IFA out of the house, claiming he was pushing a product that had already been rejected. In return, the IFA complained that he'd done lots of work and got nothing in return.

I referred a solicitor to someone on Ecademy who needed conveyancing on a number of properties. A few months later, I had a message from the Ecademist claiming the solicitor had 'ripped them off'. I spoke to the solicitor, who said the Ecademist was a 'predator'.

I was relieved that none of these people held me responsible, but it did make me reluctant to refer them again.

On the other hand, I've been involved with referrals that have gone spectacularly well.

When referrals go right

An Ecademist asked if I knew someone who could raise £1m against unpaid invoices. That's right, one million pounds! I never thought I'd pass a million-pound referral, but I did know the exact person to help. It was an ex-BRX member who did factoring. He'd been a member for two years and had never got a referral even though he'd done everything right – he'd turned up at every meeting, explained what he did, and given referrals to others. I'd met him a few times and remembered him, so when the occasion arose, I was able to make the introduction. I know it worked out, because I was paid an introducer's commission and they both took me to lunch to thank me.

A client asked me to write a fund-raising proposal for them. It's not the kind of writing I do, so I posted an appeal on Ecademy for a specialist. A couple of people in my network recommended a particular individual, so I put him in touch with my client. Again, I know it worked out because the Ecademist subscribed me to the wonderful Hotel Chocolat tasting club (which meant a box of delicious chocolates dropped through my door every month for three months), while the client promised me a Christmas hamper. All it took from me was a couple of emails!

I heard a story when I visited BNI about a copper roofer, who'd been a member for a couple of years and never had a referral. Obviously, it's a very specialised business and not very easy to refer! One of his chapter members was having lunch in central London when he overheard a conversation on the next table about re-roofing the church. He leaned over and asked: "Do you need a copper roofer?" And the roofer got £250,000 of business, just because his colleague was in the right place at the right time, with his 'ears open' for opportunities. By the way, I kept the business card for that roofer – it's made of copper!

An accountant referred me to a client who needed help with his brochure. I wrote the copy and referred the client to a photographer and search engine experts that he also needed. We did all the work but the accountant got all the credit!

Having networked for so long, I now get referrals, repeat business and second, third or even fourth and fifth-generation referrals.

Pass it on

I went to one BNI meeting when I first started my business, and met a photographer who recommended me to an accountant who needed help with his newsletter. I wrote and designed newsletters for the accountant for a couple of years until the partnership broke up. He then recommended me to a telecoms company. I produced newsletters for them for nearly five years, until they downsized. Six months later, they recommended me to another telecoms company. The original accountant has also come back for more work. All because I went to one breakfast meeting, on one occasion!

That was lucky – you don't often get a referral the first time you meet someone. It's unlikely that someone who's just met you would say: "Ooh, good, you're just what I'm looking for, let me give you the money in my pocket or pass your details to my valued contacts".

More often, it takes time to build up the relationship, to generate the understanding in what you offer and what you're looking for, to develop the trust that you deliver what you promise, and to grow the goodwill that makes people like you and want to help you. Not everyone is ever understood, trusted AND liked to the same level.

What's next for networking?

From a time when networking was hardly mentioned as a marketing tool, I've noticed an increasing number of people who have made it their full-time occupation.

One is like a freelance salesman. He takes on clients and promotes them at networking events. Another is an outsourcing hub. She has signed up a collection of preferred suppliers and passes work on to them in return for a commission. There are plenty of people who offer training in networking skills, both to small businesses and to corporates (I'm one of them!). And of course, any number of people make money by running networking events and organisations, both online and offline.

With so many networking opportunities to choose from, many networking organisations find that member numbers are dwindling, so they now include added value peer-to-peer development programmes, such as Ecademy Boardrooms and 1230 PowerHouse meetings. And with the growth of social media marketing, more and more networking is now taking place online. Find out more in my *Little Fish Guide to Social Media*.

BONUS CHAPTER: EXHIBITIONS & EVENTS

First things first

Afterwards, many exhibitors complain that there is not enough footfall, that the only people going around the exhibition are the other exhibitors, or that the only visitors are job-seekers or sales-people, not prospective clients. So, before you decide whether exhibitions are a good route to market for you at all, why not contact exhibitors from the previous year, and ask what results they achieved?

3 top tips for exhibitors

1. Consider your objective

Exhibitions are not just about winning new business. Are you taking a stand to raise your brand profile, as a networking opportunity or because it's a good place to 'see and be seen'?

2. Cost:benefit analysis

Think how many customers you need to win to get return on your investment. Include preparation time, the cost of display materials, giveaways and hand-outs, time out of the office, follow-up time.

3. Follow-ups

Don't give everything away at once, capture visitor contact details and follow-up promptly, within two weeks at the latest.

Things to remember

- You only have three seconds to make an impact
- Wear comfy shoes
- Keep smiling!

How do I make my display stand outstanding?

Many exhibitors seem to think it's OK to have display banners, A4 hand-outs, a rolling PowerPoint presentation, some branded giveaways, a bowl of sweets and a Champagne draw, just because that's how everyone else does it.

But we all know what happens when we go to an exhibition. We wander around, glancing at each stand, trying not to make eye contact with the exhibitors and thinking: 'Boring! Boring! Boring!'

If you're lucky, visitors will put their business card in your free draw, or take one of your sweeties to eat as they collect more and more promotional literature and giveaways into their carrier bags. Guess what happens when they get home? They throw away all the bumpf, eat the sweets and give the freebies to the kids.

As an exhibitor, you might be exhibiting your brand, product or service alongside your direct competitors. You want to attract people's attention so they think, 'Ooh, that looks interesting!' and come to talk to you, instead of the others.

So how do you make that happen? In my opinion, the 'best' stand is the one that says, at a glance, who you are, what you do, and why you're good at it.

Follow the advice in *The Little Fish Guide to DIY Marketing*, about being Uluru not Everest to stand out from your surroundings. Attract attention with something eye-catching. Make it interactive so there is something to involve people. Don't just offer a Champagne draw in return for collecting business cards. Offer something unique to your business. If it has to be Champagne, at least get it branded with your own logo on the label.

Word games

I was offered a display table at an event where I was guest speaker. Rather than have a stand with leaflets on and my roll-up banner behind, I decided to launch a challenge: 'Beat the Writer at Scrabble'. Throughout the day, my table was busier than anyone else's, with visitors crowded round trying to win £10 by getting a higher score than me. The results were shown on a flipchart page stuck to the wall behind me. Fortunately, no-one beat my high score so I kept my tenner! But they all went away knowing that I was a writer. Some of them picked up a business card or postcard from my table. Several contacted me afterwards for quotes. Still more signed up for my newsletter, so I can keep in touch with them every month and remind them I exist and what I do.

What could YOU do?
Think of a giveaway that is unique to your industry, your brand or your individual personality e.g. as a copywriter I might give away fridge magnet poetry. (Remember not to expect a direct return on this investment; it's just to raise goodwill and brand awareness.)

_____

_____

_____

Think of a relevant and involving activity e.g. if you are a printer, perhaps you could have a potato print competition, where visitor artwork is displayed on your stand and judged at the end of the day. (Remember your aim is to **engage** people.)

_____

_____

_____

Just like magic!

An accountant client was exhibiting at a business fair, and they invited me to proofread their handouts. They also showed me the plans for their stand, and it could easily have won a prize for The Single Most Boring Stand at the Show! So I said, "You don't want to do it like that!" and between us we changed their theme from dreary 'business transformation' to exciting 'business magic'! This prompted them to dress up as Harry Potter and hire a magician to entertain the delegates. People (attendees and fellow exhibitors) couldn't resist joining in as they walked by. This led to lots of leads for my client, as well as useful coverage in the local press.

Top tip: If you are exhibiting overseas, at least make an effort to learn a few words of the local language.

How can I be a guest speaker at networking events?

Rather than just attend a big networking event or exhibition where you can meet a handful of people at most, why not go as the guest speaker and then everyone will know who you are? By providing good value information and being seen as an expert, people are more likely to buy from you, recommend you, or at the very least, sign up for your newsletter (and maybe buy from you later!). To get invited to speak, just ask the organisers. They'll usually be glad of it. They might even pay you!

Top tip: Ensure you have something useful to say (not just a sales pitch). And say it in a creative way (not just the dreaded Death by PowerPoint).

WWWWWH

Before you prepare your speech or host your own event, first decide the answers to six key questions. These are the same questions that good journalists ask when writing any news story (look at your daily newspaper and see how they are answered in most headlines):

Why: What is the objective of the event, what is the outcome that is required?

Who: Who are the presenter(s), who makes up the audience, who can facilitate, who can help?

What: What format is required, for example, is it a meeting, an interactive workshop, a full-scale conference or something else?

When: What date(s) and time(s) will it run?

Where: In what venue or location will it happen?

How: Will any special equipment or refreshments be required?

Content
Think what 3-7 things you want the audience to know, then include them in priority order. People can't remember much more than that.

Structure
Include a beginning, a middle and an end. For example, you could write an introduction followed by detail and examples then

a conclusion or summary of key points. Or you could describe the problem, suggest a solution, then note the actions to be taken.

Opening and closing
Start with a surprise or a laugh, end on a high.

Pace and variety
Use different presentation techniques: Show-and-tell v interaction; video v still visual aids; fun v serious. Include something active for the 'graveyard' stint after the lunch break. Check WWWWWWH for each session.

Visual aids
Be creative – you can vary between words, numbers, pictures and sound, music and action. People benchmark your visual aids against TV. Video can be highly effective and has become much more affordable.

Top tip: For video presentations you can have visuals without words but not words without visuals.

How can I arrange my own events?

As well as getting yourself onto the speaker circuit for other people's events, you could run your own networking meeting, workshop, training session or seminar.

In this case, your role is to co-ordinate between the audience, any fellow presenters and any production crew. As with any kind of management, the secret of success is to make sure everyone has what they need to do their job, by clarifying what they need to do and when they need to do it.

As the event manager, it is your responsibility to book the meeting room (or delegate this task to someone else but make sure it gets done). Agree the room layout, book the furniture and organise any props that may be needed. Order refreshments. Obtain any equipment e.g. flipcharts, pens, OHP, laptop(s), projector(s), screen, extension leads. Always take a spare of everything and have printed copies available too, just in case.

For complex events, prepare a schedule and checklist of action points, with responsibilities individually allocated and deadlines. Allow plenty of time to set up, rehearse and clear away.

Before the event

You may need to arrange design and print for:

- Invitations (including maps, directions and RSVP mechanism)
- Name badges
- Agenda
- Handouts
- Goody bags
- Feedback forms

Issue invitations in advance and consider an email reminder shortly before the event. Collate the final guest list so the venue and caterers know exactly how many people to expect.

On the day, arrive early and check:

- Are the tables and chairs arranged as you want?
- Is all the equipment delivered and working?
- Can you and your visual aids be seen OK from every seat?

- Know your entrance and exit cues
- Practise speaking so you feel comfortable in the space

"Hellooo!"

I was co-speaker at a concert hall in Glasgow with an audience of about 2,000. We were all using clip mics and had done a sound check in advance. Off-stage, we'd built up our energy and excitement to such a level that when I burst onto the stage, my first word "Hello!" bellowed out so loudly that the whole audience laughed and – out of the corner of my eye – I could see the sound engineer leap to his controls to turn down the volume.

Equipment

If anything goes wrong, it is likely to be the technology, so make sure you know how to use it.

Laptop
- How do you forward slides (mouse or remote control)?
- Check compatibility with the venue (do you need an adapter)?
- Have you got an extension lead?
- Have you got a back-up plan in case of power failure?

Overhead Projector (OHP)
I haven't seen one of these in a while but there may be some people who still use them!

- Which way up do you put the slide on the projector?
- How do you switch it on and focus it?
- Practise pointing at the slide not at the screen

During the event

Try to enjoy it (but be ready for any contingency...fire bells going off, power cut, equipment breakdown, heckling, too hot, too cold, audience member being taken ill, noisy roadworks outside...).

Equipment failure

I was booked to deliver a presentation about catalogue production at a major industry conference, but then got double-booked. I emailed my assistant to ask if she'd be able to cover. She was travelling in New Zealand at the time and said 'Yes, of course' even though it was only a few days after she was due back. On the day, the projector broke down. Happily, she was unfazed. She just asked the audience to turn to their printed handouts, and worked from those while the engineers fixed the projector. She made a great impression and was congratulated afterwards for her composure.

After the event

Your role is not yet over. You are responsible for doing or delegating any clearing up that needs to be done. You probably didn't do it all on your own, so be sure to thank all your helpers. Sign off any invoices and check them against your budget.

Analyse the exit questionnaires to see how well your objective was achieved. Feedback the results to anyone involved. Finally, review the event with your team members and note all the learning for next time.

Tips for presenters

- Introduce yourself / thank the person who introduced you (perhaps write a brief biography and give it to them in advance to ensure they say the right things about you)
- Vary the pace
- Avoid jargon
- Make eye contact with the audience (using a Z-pattern from back to front is most inclusive – even if you can't see the people properly because stage lighting is in your eyes). Hold eye contact with one or two individuals from time to time for maximum impact.
- Speak s-l-o-w-l-y and clearly (nerves tend to make people speak too fast)
- Repeat any questions back so the rest of the audience can hear them
- Answer questions as you go along OR at the end of the presentation. Questions can go off track, so if you take them at the end, summarise your key points again afterwards to leave the audience with the right impression.

Panel show

I organised an event for 200 senior managers at a hotel in Euston.
As well as video and slide presentations, it included a fashion
show on roller-skates, and a 'Who Wants to be a Millionnaire'
quiz. Everything was rehearsed and went beautifully, except for
one session. The only session we couldn't prepare. The session
where the board of directors were on stage as a 'live' Q&A panel.

One of the directors turned out to have a certain nervous habit,
that of bouncing his hand up and down in his lap. Because of the
angle he was sitting, half the audience could see it was entirely
innocent, but it looked completely different to the other half!
There was a lot of giggling but nothing at all I could do except let
him know afterwards. How embarrassing!

How do I get bums on seats at my events?

If you're aiming to win sales by demonstrating your product or
expertise in a face-to-face seminar or workshop, how do you
guarantee enough attendees to make it worthwhile?

Here are a few of my favourite tips:

- Know your audience
- Choose a subject to suit them
- Think of an enticing title
- Start marketing well in advance
- Charge a proper price (people don't value what
  they get for nothing)
- Charge a deposit to avoid 'no-shows'

- Charge extra if they pay on the door (you need to know numbers in advance)
- Offer 'early bird' discounts
- Offer 'bring a friend' discounts
- Include testimonials in all your marketing
- Offer a money-back guarantee if not satisfied (to take away perceived risk)

Setting expectations

I was at an event that was going quite well, until the speaker started by saying (twice): "Oh no, my speech is going to be so boring." The audience then knew exactly what to expect, and guess what, they got it!

He wasn't the only one. I went to a presentation about sales. The presenter introduced it: "I'm sorry, but this is going to be boring. Sales is sales is sales." I thought she would then jump up and say: "Oh no, it isn't! Sales are EXCITING! They are the moment you win the business and make the money!" But she didn't. She had good open body language with a confident stance. She had a smart appearance and wore a colourful scarf that attracted attention. She had a great voice and eye contact with the whole audience. The material she'd prepared was good. But she was right, her presentation was boring.

Top tip: Stay positive! If you think your presentation is boring, rewrite it! If your presentation skills need improvement, get some training! If you don't present effectively, you won't get your message across and you are wasting everyone's time.

Visual aids

As you may know, I used to work at Freemans home shopping. I was invited to present at a supplier conference at Newmarket Racecourse. My speech was about the importance of sticking to the catalogue production schedule. One of my slides showed a dummy page with a made-up item description: *'We're sure this garment is lovely but we don't know because the supplier hasn't given us any details'*. The next slide showed a naked model posing on the beach with a censored sign across her body, to show what would happen if the bikini sample didn't arrive on time for the photo-shoot. These images got the message across without any words. During the run-through, another presenter told me: "Wow, your slides have so much impact, I don't want to go on after you!"

Visual hindrances

One presentation I attended wasn't so much 'Death by PowerPoint' as Death by Word document. The presenter just scrolled through the text and read bits of it off the screen. Yawn!

At another, the presenter didn't know how to turn on the projector once it had clicked to 'standby'. He spent a few minutes 'faffing about' trying to get it to work. I had to 'hiss' instructions to him as an off-stage prompt but he'd already lost any credibility he had with the audience. It's such a silly error that's easy to avoid.

Top tip: Visual aids should <u>enhance</u> your presentation, not destroy it!

How should I use PowerPoint for best effect?

PowerPoint can be a useful visual aid, when used properly. But too many people include too much text on each slide then read the text aloud. An experiment proves why that's a really bad idea:

Audience recall from a PowerPoint presentation was tested two days later. The best results were from those people who were left to read the slides quietly, with no commentary. Second best were people who listened to the content read aloud (with no slides). The worst results were from people who saw the slides AND heard them read at the same time.

Conclusion: The brain reads more quickly than the spoken word. If slides are read aloud, the brain gets the same message at two different speeds, causing confusion and lack of retention.

Just one more reason why PowerPoint slides should be more visual than text!

Make it sexy

When I worked in the corporate world, I was asked to design a PowerPoint presentation on behalf of someone in IT. He asked me to include a picture of a lingerie model in the middle of the presentation: 'because otherwise it would be too boring.' I refused and asked why he didn't just rewrite it to be more interesting.

Tips for PowerPoint

- Use bullet point text (an odd number looks more balanced than an even number)
- Maximum 7 lines per slide or simple visuals
- White or yellow on dark blue reads best
- Black on white is more elegant and modern
- Slides can 'build' line by line
- Slides can have animation effects
- You can print handouts for the audience and choose whether to distribute them before or after the presentation (Before means they can make notes as you go along, but they can also look ahead which may spoil any surprises you have planned. After means they have something to take away.)
- You can print out your script as 'speaker notes' (use at least 18pt type, double-spaced so it's easy to read at a distance). Give a copy to the PowerPoint operator (if you are not doing it yourself) as their cue to change slides.
- Beware the echo effect from lecterns designed to amplify sound. Turn over the page carefully as paper rustles sound like elephants in the jungle. Rest your hands on the lectern gently or it bangs like a drum.
- Don't walk around with keys or coins in your pocket as they jangle distractingly
- Don't keep hold of a pen while you talk – it's not a sword and doesn't offer any magical protection!

Top tip: Search YouTube for 'Identity 2.0 Keynote' to see the punchy 'Lessig style' of PowerPoint presentation.

Where can I get help with my public speaking skills?

Top tip: Public speaking is a good skill to develop, as it benefits your career even if you don't plan to go networking or give presentations.

The Toastmasters organisation provides a friendly and supportive learning environment, and has meetings around the world. (I've qualified as CTM Bronze.) Members work through a series of speeches that focus on different objectives such as eye contact, structure, vocal variety and body language. As well as prepared speeches, you can practice impromptu speaking, and also get the chance to enter local, national and international competitions. At advanced level, you can work on specialist speeches, such as humour or story-telling. At every meeting, you get support from other members in a 'positive feedback sandwich' i.e. what you did well, what you might try next time, and something else they enjoyed about your speech.

You don't just learn key public speaking skills, you also meet some fantastic people, get an insight into their lives, discover new things, have a laugh, and sometimes even get a tear in your eye. Search 'Toastmasters District 71' to find all UK clubs. You may also wish to check out the ASC (Association of Speakers Clubs) and the PSA (Professional Speaking Association).

Top tip: Use silence to replace filler words such as um, er, but, basically and y'know.

Our souls

When I was at school, I was quite shy. I didn't often contribute to class discussions. One day, in Religious Education class, the teacher asked a question that I actually had an opinion about, so I put up my hand. Of course, she picked on me to answer. The question was about whether animals have souls. I started a long spiel about 'our souls and their souls', and one by one my classmates started laughing. I didn't know why so I just carried on talking about 'their souls and our souls', until eventually even the teacher was laughing and I finally realised what I was saying. I learned that what the audience hear is not necessarily what you think you said. (Read this story aloud and it will make sense!)

Attention-grabbing

While studying for my Open University degree, I volunteered as an OUSA rep* at summer school. That meant I organised social, marketing and fund-raising events for around 450 students on campus for a week each year. Once, I had to give a keynote speech at Sussex University, alongside a particularly handsome fellow rep. I thought I'd done a fine job, getting my message across clearly and with humour. However, lots of the (female) students came up to me afterwards, to apologise, saying: "I'm sure your speech was fabulous but I couldn't pay any attention because I was so captivated by the bloke standing next to you."

* Open University Students' Assocation representative

Breaking the ice

I believe that a fun introduction that makes people laugh is the best way to get any event off to a good start. Here are some of my favourite ideas, all tried and tested and known to work!

1. Pass the parcel

The game works just like the kids' version but you put a question to be answered in each layer of the parcel to be unwrapped. They can be business questions e.g. 'Describe your ideal client' or social e.g. 'What was your best-ever holiday?' You can also put little prizes in, sweets etc., perhaps with a bigger prize in the middle e.g. desk diary or the entrance fee refunded.

You can probably take your own CD player and CD/s, but better check this is OK with the venue in case you need a Public Performance Licence (PPL) and ensure any electrical equipment you provide has an up-to-date Portable Appliance Testing (PAT) label. Also take an extension lead in case it's needed to reach the power supply, plus tape to stick any wires safely to the floor.

2. Networking bingo

This works best for groups of 20 or more.

In advance...
Prepare a 'bingo sheet'. Down the left hand column, list various characteristics of the people you expect to attend, e.g. 'solicitor' or 'has blue eyes'. Leave a corresponding space down the right hand column. You can choose whatever categories you wish, as serious or silly as appropriate. Copy / print enough so there is a bingo sheet for everybody (plus a few over just in case). You may

need to bring a supply of pens as well. Amazingly, some people attend networking meetings without one!

On the day...
Allow 10 minutes (yes, just 10 minutes!) for people to collect as many signatures as they can on their bingo sheet. One person can only sign once on any page, and you cannot sign your own. The first person to collect 20 different signatures wins the prize. (If it's a paid event, I give away a bottle of Champagne / wine with my business card on a tag round the bottle-neck. If it's a free event, I give away the chance to present your business for one-minute to the audience so they all know who you are and what you do).

If you run out of time, the person with the most signatures wins (count down from 20, 19, 18 etc.).

Optional extras...
You can insist that they exchange business cards along with signatures. You can go through the list afterwards with a show of hands so everyone can see who in the whole audience qualifies for each category.

The benefits...
It's a great ice-breaker, people can get really competitive and start climbing over chairs to collect signatures! It's not 'proper networking' but you do learn a little something about other people and find random connections to follow up later.

3. Pennies in a basket
Source: Cedar Events Organisers www.cedar-events.co.uk

Works for any number of attendees. Give everyone 10 x 1p coins, and put an empty basket (or other receptacle) in the centre of the table. Go round the table with everyone in turn saying something they have **never** done. If other people **have** done that thing, they put a penny in the basket. Keep going round until whoever runs out of pennies first is the winner, for being the most adventurous person in the room. Get all the other pennies back and you won't even be out of pocket!

4. Warm fuzzies

A good way of breaking a big group into smaller ones. You get the fluffy balls from craft shops, about 20 for £1. Everyone takes a ball when they arrive, creating a nice sense of anticipation. On the organiser's instruction, they have to find the other people with the same size and colour balls(!). They then present to their small groups for one minute each, saying who they are, what they do, why they are good at it, and what they are looking for. You need a whistle or gong to make a loud noise every 60 seconds to keep it moving along.

5. Key words

You can also create mixed groups by putting an index card on each person's chair with a key word written on it. The key words are in groups of 5 (or whatever) but placed randomly round the room e.g. things to do with hamburgers, superheroes, soap stars etc. It's interesting to see who chooses to sit where when they read the card on the seat!

On your command, people have to find the others in their group (although I've had people trying to match Julia Roberts with whipped cream before!). Each sub-group must find one thing they all have in common e.g. been up the Eiffel Tower, born in Croydon, have blue eyes.

6. More ways to make sub-groups

Write pairs (or more) of animals on cards. Everyone picks a card at random, and then has to find their 'mate/s' by making animal noises only.

OR

Stick a Post-It™ note on everyone's forehead naming one of a famous couple or members of a group. They have to ask questions with Yes/No answers only to identify themselves and find their matching partner/s e.g. Queen Victoria & Prince Albert, Tom & Jerry, Posh & Scary & Baby & Sporty & Ginger.

OR

Stick a coloured sticker on everyone's name badge at registration. Ask people to find those with a matching sticker and introduce themselves to each other.

6. Snowball fight

Each person writes their name and two unusual facts about themselves on a piece of paper. Then screw all the pieces of paper into 'snowballs' and throw them to each other. General mayhem ensues!

After a few moments, you stop the throwing, and everyone has to find the person who wrote the page they are holding. They then have to find out one other unusual fact about that person.

Finally, they introduce the other person (and their three facts) to the rest of the group.

One man read out "I'm pregnant" to the consternation of
everyone in the room. He was reading the 'snowball' thrown by
one of the women who chose this way to reveal her expectations!
Source: Andy Lopata

7. Categories

Works best when people already know each other a bit.

Ask a defining question e.g. "If you were an animal what would you be and why?" Everyone (including you) answers the question in turn. Then the next person chooses a category e.g. "If you were a meal what would you be and why?" and everyone answers that. Continue until each person has chosen a category.

8. Truth or lies

Great for people who don't know each other very well.

Go round the table and each person says three things about themselves, two must be true and the other a lie. The rest have to guess the lie.

9. Pig personality profile

Ask each participant to draw a pig on a Post-It™ note. When they've finished, stick them all on the wall as a 'gallery' and invite everyone round to admire them (so this ice-breaker is not suitable for larger groups). Tell them it's similar to a Myers-Briggs personality test (but stress it isn't really, it's just a bit of fun).

Here's the interpretation of the drawings – it's interesting to see whether anybody owns up to any of the traits described:

- If the pig is drawn towards the top of the paper,
  you are a positive and optimistic person.
- If the pig is drawn towards the middle of the page,
  you are a realist.
- If the pig is drawn towards the bottom of the page,
  you are a pessimist and have a tendency to behave
  negatively.
- If the pig is facing left,
  you believe in tradition, are friendly and remember
  dates and birthdays.
- If the pig is facing towards the viewer,
  you are direct, enjoy playing devil's advocate and
  neither fear nor avoid discussion.
- If the pig is facing right,
  you are innovative and active, but have neither a sense
  of family nor remember dates.
- If the pig is drawn with many details,
  you are analytical, cautious and distrustful.
- If the pig is drawn with few details,
  you are emotional, naïve, care little for detail and take
  risks.
- If the pig is drawn with four legs showing,
  you are secure, stubborn and stick to your ideals.
- If the pig is drawn with fewer than four legs showing,
  you are insecure or are living through a period of major
  change.
- The larger the pig's ears are drawn,
  the better listener you are.
- The longer the pig's tail you have drawn,
  the more satisfied you are with the quality of your
  social/sex life!

10. Name games

Go round the room getting each person to introduce themselves in turn by name, and business name

PLUS

State who you would ideally like to bring your pyjamas to you, if you were in hospital

OR

...Add an alliterative adjective e.g. Awesome Annie (you can turn this into a memory game where the next person has to repeat all the names and adjectives that have gone before as well as introducing themselves – it helps people remember new names and characteristics)

OR

...Give the name of your first pet and the road where you live. This gives your film star (or porn star!) name.

Note: some people suggest using mother's maiden names for this but others are reluctant to do so as they are often used as online passwords.

11.Fascinating facts

Pass round a roll of toilet paper. Everyone takes as many sheets as they like, but then they have to tell the group a fact about themselves equal to the number of sheets they took.

OR

Prepare a list of facts about each person with a copy to all. Ask each person one yes/no question until each fact is claimed.

OR

In turn say: 'The sun shines on people who x' (must be true about yourself). All who do that thing move to another chair. Remove chairs one by one until only one person is left seated.

12.Speed networking

Get the group to form two circles, the inner ring facing the outer ring in pairs.

People in the inner circle have one minute to tell their partner about their business – what they do, why they are good at it, and what referrals they are looking for.

The person in the outer circle has one minute to do the same. Both people then share ideas of how they can help each other. Blow a whistle (or bang a gong or hoot a party honker), and the people in the outer circle move round one place clockwise to make a new pairing.

OR

Set out tables with opposite pairs of seats, to match the number of attendees. One person (the 'keystone') remains in their chair throughout, the others all move one place to the left each time (this ensures everybody eventually gets to speak to everybody else at the event).

If there is an odd number of attendees, place a 'rest break' notice in one place and move it along every time.

Note: You WILL need a timer/stopwatch, you WILL need something to make a loud noise and keep it moving along over all the talking, you WILL need to provide refreshments so attendees don't end up losing their voices. One hour is more than enough (that's 40 people having 20 conversations of 3 minutes each).

13.Get knotted

The whole group forms a large circle and slowly walks to the centre.

Everyone should now try to hold hands with two other people across the circle.

When there are no free hands, the leader breaks the link between two people and the group have to untangle themselves into a line - without talking.

14.Load of balls
Source: Simon Raybould www.curved-vision.co.uk

Sit people around a table and get each one to write their initials on a ping-pong ball. When the game starts, each person at the same time bounces their ball onto the table to be caught by the person opposite who bounces it back to the person to the left of the original. General chaos ensues as balls go everywhere!

After a short period of time you stop the chaos and people have to quickly find out whose ball they have and ask them one question. They've only got 30 seconds to do this (with everyone talking at once) before you start the ball bouncing again.

Repeat until you've had enough.

About the author

Jackie Barrie runs Comms Plus, the writing and design agency that specialises in making complex information appear simple.

Her marketing experience comes from nearly three decades in the industry, spanning copywriting, graphic design, print, web design, sales promotion, brand identity and much more!

She grew the business from nothing, reducing her marketing budget to zero (nil, nada, zilch) because 98% of her work now comes from repeat business and referral recommendations. It's ironic, because 'traditional' marketing is the main service she provides to her clients, yet she no longer needs to do very much of it herself.

Her 'big fish' corporate clients have included: FirstPlus, Tesco, Ann Summers, PricewaterhouseCoopers, Domestic & General Insurance PLC, Freemans and Grattan. Her 'little fish' SME (small & medium enterprise) clients range from accounts to recruitment and telecoms to training, with a sprinkling of sole traders in between.

Before founding Comms Plus in 2001, Jackie worked her way up to Senior Manager level in the corporate world, with a team of 12 graphic designers and copywriters reporting to her. Some of her notable achievements include:

- Recommended stationery redesigns saving over £500K p.a.
- Managed purchasing contract worth £3m p.a.
- Organised fun day which raised over £5K for Save the Children Fund

- Co-ordinated design and print of stationery to launch a new brand
- Reduced the number of stock letters used from 864 to 537 and rewrote them to fit new house style, so reducing customer complaints about unhelpful letters by one-third

Jackie has also worked as an insurance clerk, a bar-maid and a tea-lady.

Her favourite aspect of employment was having an MGF as a company car. Her favourite aspect of self-employment is not having to ask anyone for a day off.

She holds a BA Hons degree in psychology, both social – what makes people tick – and cognitive – the mental processes people go through when they read words and symbols on paper or on screen. She is also a qualified NLP Practitioner, and is particularly fascinated by the language of influence.

She hates tomatoes, alarm clocks and shoes, and likes dancing, scuba diving and making people laugh.

You'll find more of Jackie's tips at **www.comms-plus.co.uk**, on **Ezine Articles** and at **http://jackiebarrie.blogspot.com**. You'll also find her on social networking sites including **LinkedIn** and **Facebook**, and can follow her on Twitter **@jackiebarrie**. You can phone her on **0845 899 0258** or email **jackie@comms-plus.co.uk**.

YOUR NOTES